Christian Megahits

The Ultimate Sheet Music Collection

Produced by
Alfred Music Publishing Co., Inc.
P.O. Box 10003
Van Nuys, CA 91410-0003
alfred.com

Printed in USA.

ISBN-10: 0-7390-9109-3
ISBN-13: 978-0-7390-9109-8

Cover Photos
Silhouette: © iStockphoto / nopow • Piano Keys: © iStockphoto / Alexey Bushtruk
Burst Background: © iStockphoto / hfng • Squares Background: © istockphoto / Tomasz Sowinski

 Alfred Cares. Contents printed on 100% recycled paper.

Contents

10,000 Reasons
(Bless the Lord)

Words and Music by
MATT REDMAN and JONAS MYRIN

6

Verse 1 (Sing 1st time only):

Verse 2 (Sing 2nd time only):

wor-ship Your ho - ly name.___

1. The
2. You're

sun comes up, it's a new day dawn - ing.___ It's time to sing Your song___

rich in love and You're slow to an - ger. Your name is great, and Your

___ a - gain.___ What - ev - er may___ pass and what - ev - er lies be -

heart is kind.___ For all Your good-ness, I will___ keep on

8

Chorus:

Sing like nev - er be - fore, oh, my soul. I

wor-ship Your ho - ly name.___ Je - sus, I will wor-ship Your ho - ly name,___

wor - ship Your ho - ly name.___

ABOVE ALL

Words and Music by
PAUL BALOCHE
and LENNY LEBLANC

Above All - 4 - 1

14

ALIVE (MARY MAGDALENE)

Words and Music by
BERNIE HERMS
and NICOLE NORDEMAN

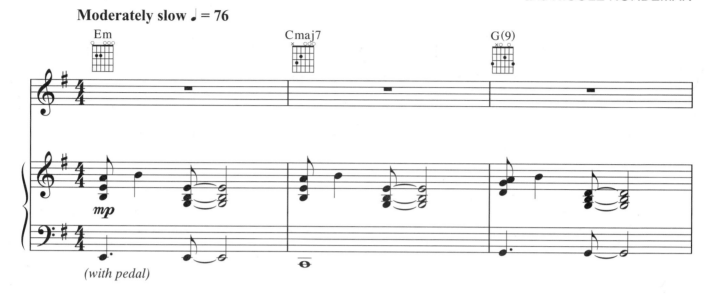

18

22

Chorus:

A - live!_____ A - live!_____ Look what mer-

cy's o - ver-come. Death has lost and love has__ won._____

A - live!

Yeah,_____ I am His___ be - cause He__

AMAZING GRACE
(My Chains Are Gone)

Words and Music by
CHRIS TOMLIN and LOUIE GIGLIO

Amazing Grace - 5 - 1

Verse 2:

Verse 3:

Verse 4:

shall soon dis-solve_____ like snow,_ the sun___ for-bear to shine. But_ God, who_ called_ me here be-low,_ will be for-ev - er mine,___ will be_____ for - ev - er mine._

decresc. poco a poco

You are for-ev - er mine.

rit.

ALL THIS TIME

Words and Music by
BEN GLOVER, DAVID GARCIA
and BRITT NICOLE

31

All This Time - 6 - 2

BETTER THAN A HALLELUJAH

Words and Music by
CHAPIN HARTFORD and SARAH HART

Better Than a Hallelujah - 6 - 1

Chorus:

pour out our mis-er-ies, God just hears a mel-o-dy. Beau-

ti-ful, the mess we are. The hon-est cries of break-ing hearts

are bet-ter than a hal-le-lu-jah.

Guitar solo:

Chorus:

We___ pour out___ our mis-er-ies,___ God___ just hears a mel-o-dy.

Beau-ti - ful,___ the mess we are.___ The hon - est cries___ of break - ing hearts___

are bet - ter than a hal - le - lu - jah.___

BLESSINGS

Words and Music by
LAURA MIXON STORY

We pray for_ Your might - y hand_ to ease our_ suf - fer - ing. And

all the while,_ You hear each spo - ken need,_ yet

love is way_ too much_ to give us less - er things._ 'Cause what if Your bless-

Chorus:

ings come_though rain - drops? What if Your heal - ing comes_through tears?_ What if a thou-

46

Bridge:

When friends be - tray___ us, when dark - ness seems___ to win,__ we__ know that pain__ re - minds__ this heart__ that this is not,___ this is not__ our home.___ It's not__ our__ home.___

BUSTED HEART (HOLD ON TO ME)

Words and Music by
BEN GLOVER, JENNA TORRES,
LUKE SMALLBONE and JOEL SMALLBONE

Moderate rock ♩ = 100

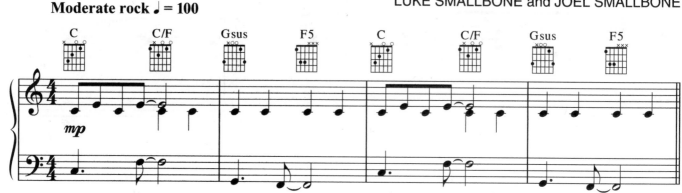

Verse 1:

1. Win-ter has come back a-gain,____ feels like the sea-son won't end. My faith is dy-in' to-night,

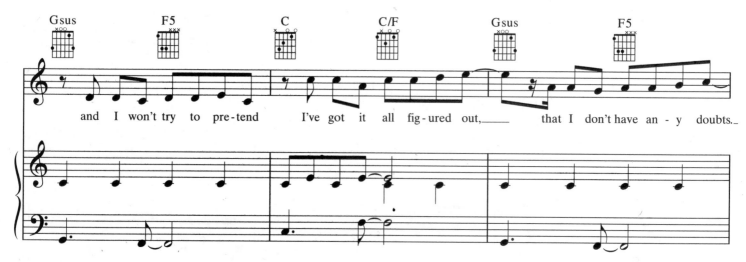

and I won't try to pre-tend I've got it all fig-ured out,____ that I don't have an-y doubts.__

Busted Heart - 7 - 1

Verse 2:

Hold on to me.

I am the wan-der-ing son; Your love was nev-er e-nough.

I keep chas-in' the wind in-stead of chas-in' Your love.

I'm scream-in' out Your name; don't let me fall on my face.

54

Bridge:

Broke Your heart a thou - sand___ times, but You nev-er left___ my___ side.

You have al - ways been___ here___ for me, mmm.___

You nev-er let___ me go.___

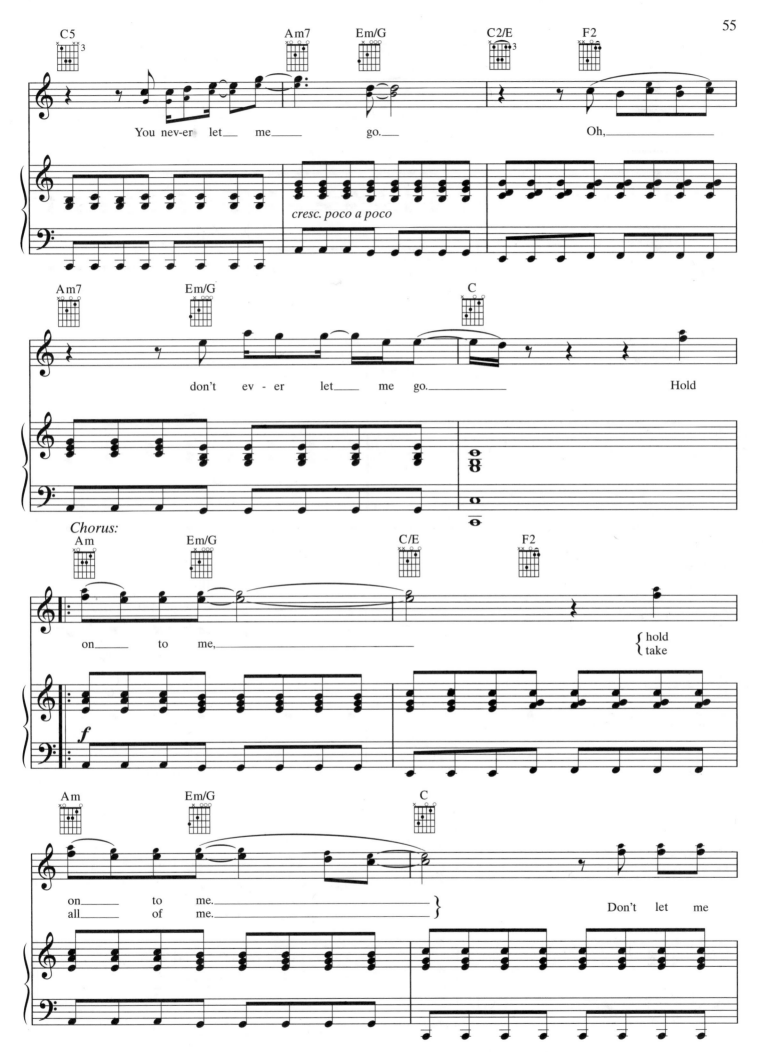

CINDERELLA

Words and Music by
STEVEN CURTIS CHAPMAN

58

Cinderella - 9 - 2

Verse 2:

62

Cinderella - 9 - 7

64

soon   the clock will   strike___   mid - night___

and   she'll   be

gone.___

CARRY ME TO THE CROSS

Words and Music by
JASON WALKER, NICK DePARTEE
and MARK STUART

Moderately slow rock ♩ = 74

Verse 1:

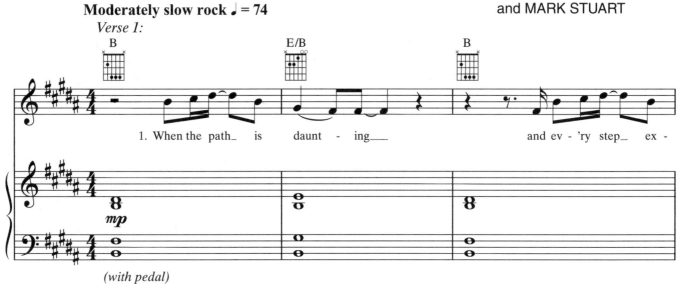

1. When the path is daunt - ing and ev - 'ry step ex -

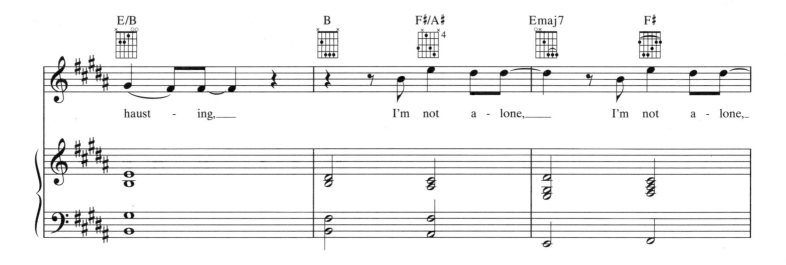

haust - ing, I'm not a - lone, I'm not a - lone,

Verse 2:

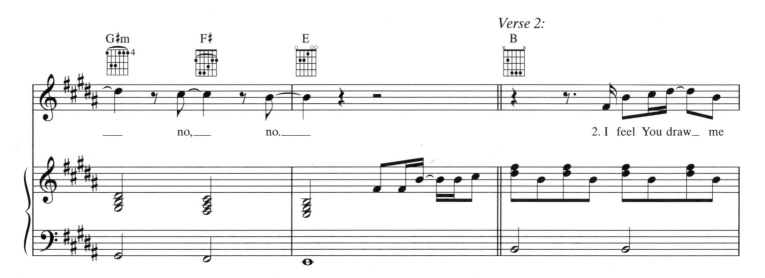

no, no. 2. I feel You draw me

Carry Me to the Cross - 6 - 1

68

71

Carry Me to the Cross - 6 - 6

CHRIST IS RISEN

Words and Music by
MATT MAHER and MIA FIELDES

CITY ON OUR KNEES

Words and Music by
CARY BARLOWE, TOBY McKEEHAN
and JAMIE MOORE

If you got-ta start some-where, why not here?

If you got-ta start some-time, why not now?

City on Our Knees - 7 - 1

City on Our Knees - 7 - 2

Chorus:

84

COURAGEOUS

Words and Music by
MATTHEW WEST and MARK HALL

Courageous - 7 - 1

86

88

Courageous - 7 - 4

DEPENDENCE

Words and Music by
JAMIE SLOCUM

Moderately slow ♩ = 80

(with pedal)

Verse 1:

1. This is the life I've al-ways want - ed,_____

to know__ the Prince of Peace,__

Dependence - 6 - 1

Chorus:

hope to car - ry on._____ You're the one thing that I can turn to.

Just to know, just to know that You're with me__ on all these roads_ I trav - el on._

__ You're the one thing that I can turn to. Just to know, just to know that You love me_

gives me hope____ to car - ry on._____ There's noth - ing this

GLORIOUS DAY
(Living He Loved Me)

Words and Music by
MARK HALL and MICHAEL BLEECKER

Rock ballad ♩ = 76

Verse 1:

(Male:) 1. One day when heav-en was filled with His prais-es, one day when sin___ was as black as could be,___ Je-sus came_ forth_ ___ to be born of a vir-gin, dwelt a-mong_ men,___ my ex-am-ple is He.___

Verses 2 & 3:

ing; O glo-ri-ous day,___ O glo-ri-ous___ day.

(Male:) 2. One day they led___ Him up Cal-va-ry's___ moun-
(Female:) 3. One day the grave___ could con-ceal Him___ no lon-

tain. One day they nailed___ Him to die on a tree.___
ger. One day the stone___ rolled a-way from the door.___

Suf-fer-ing___ an - guish, de-spised and re-ject-
Then He a-rose,___ o - ver death He had con-

Glorious Day - 7 - 3

104

Chorus:

Glorious Day - 7 - 7

I WILL RISE

Words and Music by
**CHRIS TOMLIN, JESSE REEVES,
LOUIE GIGLIO and MATT MAHER**

Moderately slow ♩ = 84

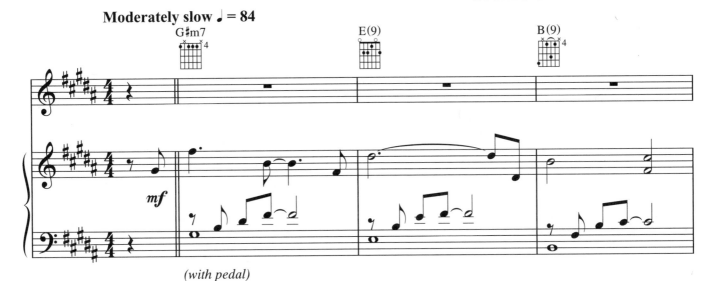

(with pedal)

Verse 1:

1. There's a peace I've come to know, though my

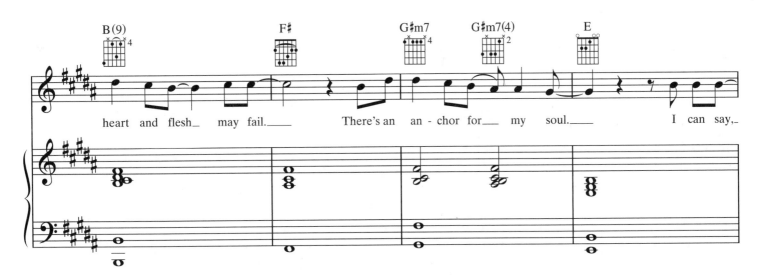

heart and flesh may fail. There's an an-chor for my soul. I can say,

I Will Rise - 7 - 1

I Will Rise - 7 - 5

110

HELD

Words and Music by
CHRISTA WELLS

Held - 8 - 1

116

Bridge:

ev - 'ry - thing fell, we'd be held._____

If hope is born of____ suf - fer - ing,

if this is on - ly____ the be - gin - ing, can we not

wait for one____ hour, watch - ing for our_____ Sav -

HOLD ME

Words and Music by
CHRIS STEVENS, JAMIE GRACE
and TOBY McKEEHAN

Moderately bright reggae feel ♩ = 136

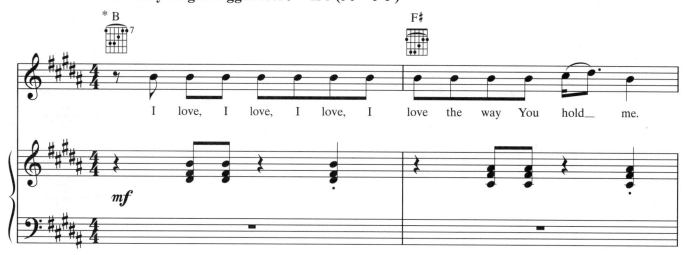

* Guitar capo at 4th fret.

E
world is gon - na bring me down, that's when Your smile_ comes a - round. Ooh, I love the way You
fig - ure You out,__ You make me wan - na sing and shout. I love the way You
Chorus:
B
F♯
G♯m7
hold me. By__ my side You'll al - ways be. You take each and ev - 'ry day, make it spe - cial in__
E
B
F♯
__ some way. I love the way You hold me. In__ Your arms I'll al - ways be. You take each and ev -

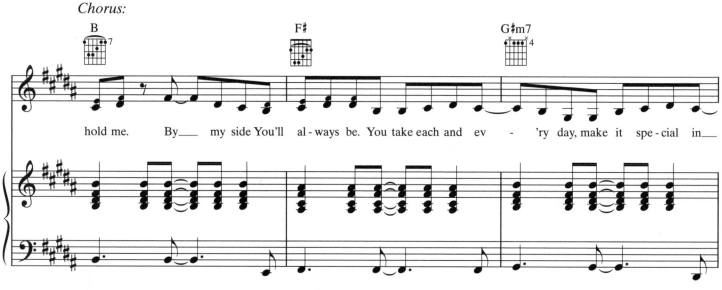

Chorus:

HOW BEAUTIFUL

Words and Music by
TWILA PARIS

Slowly and gently ♩ = 112

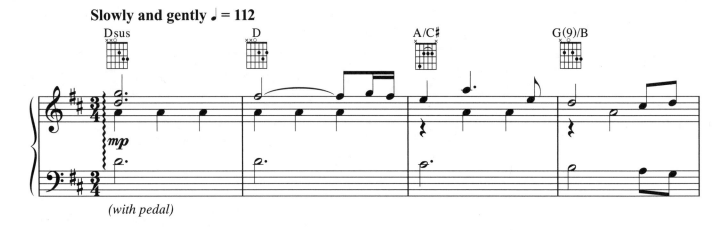

(with pedal)

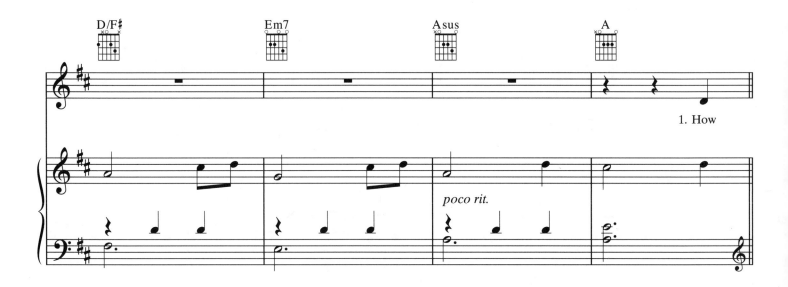

1. How

Verse 1:

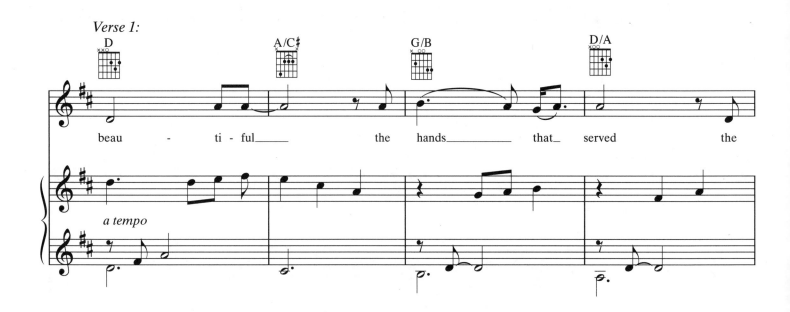

beau - ti - ful____ the hands_____ that_ served the

a tempo

How Beautiful - 10 - 4

135

How Beautiful - 10 - 8

HOW GREAT IS OUR GOD

Words and Music by
JESSE REEVES, CHRIS TOMLIN
and ED CASH

Moderately slow acoustic rock ♩ = 76

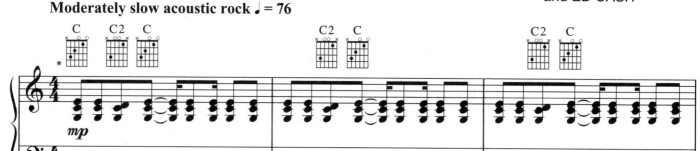

Verse 1 (sing 1st time only):

Guitar cont. simile

1. The splen-dor of_____ the King,_____

Verse 2 (sing 2nd time only):

age to age,_____ He stands,_____ and

(play l.h. 2nd time)

clothed in maj - es-ty;_____ let all the earth_ re-joice,_____ all the earth_ re-joice._

time is in_____ His hands;_____ Be-gin-ning and_ the End,_____ Be-gin-ning and_ the End._

*Original recording in D major with Guitar Capo 1.

139

How great_   How great_

_ is our God!_   Sing with me:_ How great   is our God!_

_ And all_____ will see how great,   how great___ is our God.___

HOW HE LOVES

Words and Music by
JOHN MARK MCMILLAN

Moderately ♩. = 50

Verse 1:

1. He is___ jea - lous for me,___ loves like a hur - ri - cane,

I am a tree___ bend - ing be - neath___ the weight of His wind and

144

How He Loves - 8 - 3

146

How He Loves - 8 - 5

He is our prize,_____ drawn to re-demp-tion by the grace in His eyes._ If His

grace is an o-cean, we're all sink-ing._____

And heav-en meets earth like an un-fore-seen kiss and my

heart turns vio-lent-ly in-side of my chest. I don't have time to main-

Chorus:

How He Loves - 8 - 7

I CAN ONLY IMAGINE

Words and Music by
BART MILLARD

*Play l.h. Bass cues 2nd time (on D.S.).

I Can Only Imagine - 8 - 4

I Can Only Imagine - 8 - 5

156

I LIFT MY HANDS

Words and Music by
CHRIS TOMLIN, LOUIE GIGLIO and MATT MAHER

I Lift My Hands - 6 - 2

I Lift My Hands - 6 - 6

I WILL BE HERE

Words and Music by
STEPHEN CURTIS CHAPMAN

1. To-mor-row morn-in', if you___ wake up___ and the sun does not___ ap-pear,
2. To-mor-row morn-in', if you___ wake up___ and the fu-ture is___ un-clear,

I Will Be Here - 6 - 1

165

I Will Be Here - 6 - 2

Chorus:

168

I Will Be Here - 6 - 5

I'M WITH YOU
(Ruth and Naomi)

Words and Music by
BERNIE HERMS and
NICHOLE NORDEMAN

I'm With You - 9 - 1

Chorus:

me and you,___ where you go,_____ I'll__ go too.__ I'm__ with you.__

I'm__ with you._____ 'Til your heart_

finds a home,__ I won't let____ you feel__ a - lone.__ I'm__ with you.__

I'm__ with you,_____ with_ you._____

I'm With You - 9 - 4

174

I'm With You - 9 - 5

Chorus:

IN CHRIST ALONE

Words and Music by
STUART TOWNEND
and KEITH GETTY

184

Verse 4:

life,   no fear in death;   this is the pow'r of Christ   in me.   From life's first

cry   to fi - nal breath,   Je - sus com-mands my des - ti - ny.   No pow'r of

hell,   no scheme of __ man   can ev - er pluck   me from His hand.   'Til He re - turns __

4. No guilt in

IN MY ARMS

Words and Music by
TIFFANY LEE ARBUCKLE,
MATT BRONLEEWE and JEREMY BOSE

*Original recording in E♭ minor.

In My Arms - 5 - 1

In My Arms - 5 - 2

Bridge:

Cas - tles, they__ might crum - ble.

Dreams may not__ come true.__ But you are nev - er all

a - lone, 'cause I will al - ways,_____

al - ways love__ you._____

190

In My Arms - 5 - 5

OH HAPPY DAY

Words and Music by
EDWIN R. HAWKINS

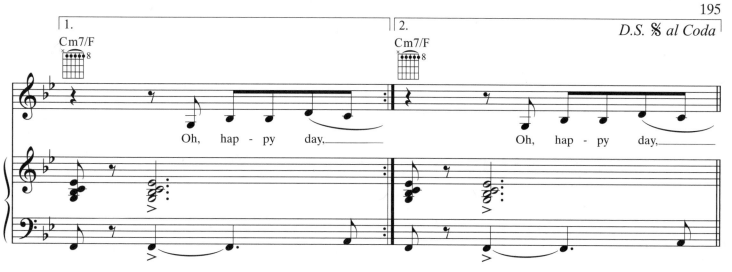

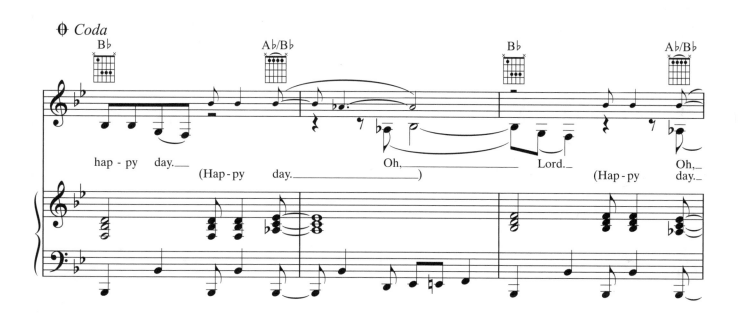

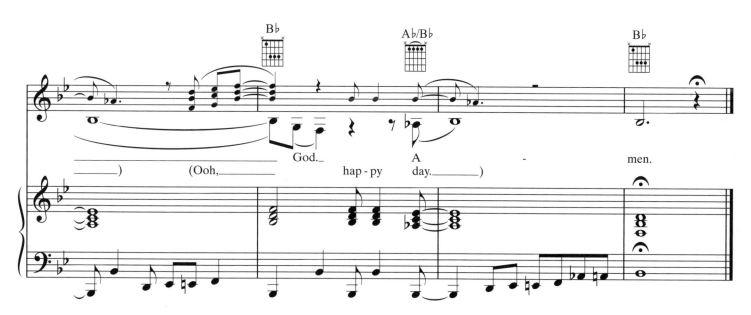

LEAD ME

Words and Music by
CHRIS ROHMAN, JASON INGRAM
and MATT HAMMITT

𝄋 *Chorus 1 & 2:*

know we___ call___ this our home,___ but I___ still feel___

To Coda ⊕

a - lone."___

Verse 2:

2. I see their fac - es; look in their in - no - cent eyes.___ They're just chil - dren

from the out - side. I'm work-ing hard; I tell my - self they'll be fine.___

200

Chorus 3:

Won't You lead___ me___ to

lead them___ with strong hands,___ to stand up___ when they can't?___ Don't want to leave___ them___ hun-gry for love,___ chas-ing___ things that I could give___ up. I'll show them___ I'm

will-ing to fight _____ and give them _____ the best of my life, so

we _____ can _____ call this our home. _____ Lead _____ me, _____ 'cause I _____

_____ can't do _____ this a - lone. _____ Fa - ther, lead_

_____ me, _____ 'cause I _____ can't do _____ this a - lone. _____

LEARNING TO BE THE LIGHT

Words and Music by
RICHARD MOORE, JOEL PARISIEN,
MARK ROGERS and JOSHUA TOAL

Moderately slow ♩ = 80

Verse 1 (sing first time only):

1. When the stars came crash-ing down in ti-ny piec-es to the ground,

Verse 2 (sing second time only):

2. When a heart is cold as ice, you can't melt it with ad-vice.

I was all a-lone down here, trapped be-neath the at-mos-phere. Then I

No one wants to lis-ten to a list of things they should-n't do. So I

Bridge:

that makes_ the shad - ows hide,_ the light that breaks_ the curse_ of pride,_ the

light that takes_ the wear - y in_ its arms._

When_ it all_ came crash-ing down,_ there was on - ly dark - ness all a - round._ But

D.S. %% al Coda

in the dis - tance, I_ could see_ a flame._ It's

LET THE CHURCH SAY AMEN

Words and Music by
ANDRAÉ CROUCH

Let the Church Say Amen - 10 - 2

210

213

214

216

217

Let the Church Say Amen - 10 - 10

MIGHTY TO SAVE

Words and Music by
REUBEN MORGAN
and BEN FIELDING

* The original recording is in F♯ major. This arrangement is raised a 1/2 step to G major, to provide a simpler key.

**Play cue notes in left hand 2nd time only.

Mighty to Save - 6 - 1

220

222 *Chorus:*

ONLY HOPE

Words and Music by
JONATHAN FOREMAN

*Original recording in C# minor.

226

OVERCOME

Words and Music by
JON EGAN

Verse 1:

1. Seat-ed a - bove, en-throned in the Fath - er's love,___

233

Overcome - 11 - 3

praise,_____ You o - ver - came.__

Je - sus, awe-some in pow - er for - ev - er. Awe-some and great is Your

name,_____ You o - ver - came.__

Verse 2:

2. Pow-er in hand, speak-ing the Fath-er's plan, You're

send-ing us out, light in this bro-ken land. All au-

thor - i - ty, ev-'ry vic-to - ry is

Overcome - 11 - 5

Chorus:

Yours._____ Sav - ior, wor-thy of hon-or and glo - ry, wor-thy of all our praise,_____ You o - ver-came.__

___ Je - sus, awe-some in pow-er for - ev - er. Awe-some and great is Your name,_____ You o - ver-came.__

Je - sus, awe - some in pow - er for - ev - er. Awe - some and great is Your name,_____ You o - ver - came.___ You o - ver - came. You o - ver - came._____

Lead vocal ad lib.

You o - ver - came.___ You o - ver - came.__

Sav - ior,

wor - thy of hon - or and glo - ry, wor - thy of all our

praise,___ You o - ver - came.__

all our praise, You o - ver came.__

THE PRAYER

Italian Lyric by
ALBERTO TESTA and TONY RENIS

Words and Music by
CAROLE BAYER SAGER and DAVID FOSTER

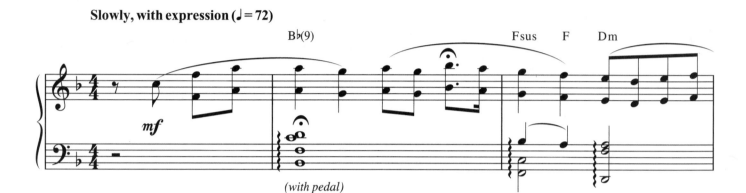

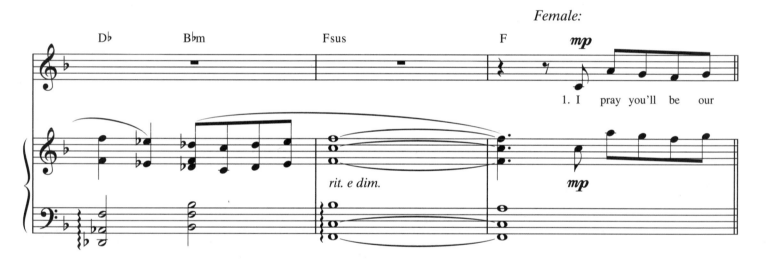

243

The Prayer - 8 - 2

244

246

The Prayer - 8 - 5

Verse 3:

248

The Prayer - 8 - 7

REVELATION SONG

Words and Music by
JENNIE LEE RIDDLE

Verse 2: (Sing first time only)

Verse 3: (Sing second time only)

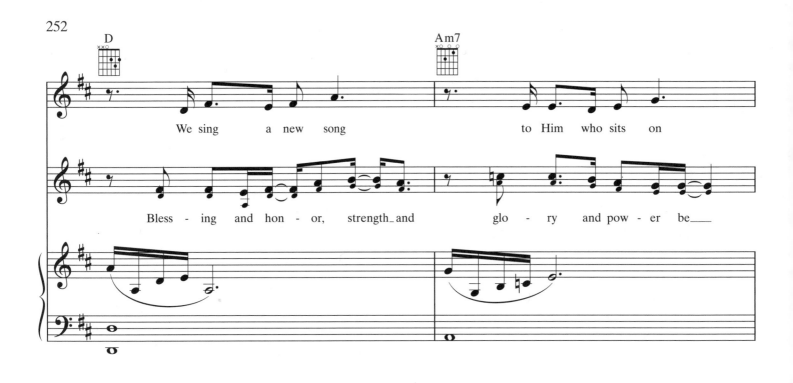

We sing a new song to Him who sits on

Bless - ing and hon - or, strength and glo - ry and pow - er be___

heav - en's mer - cy___ seat.___

to You,___ the on - ly wise_____ King.___

Chorus:

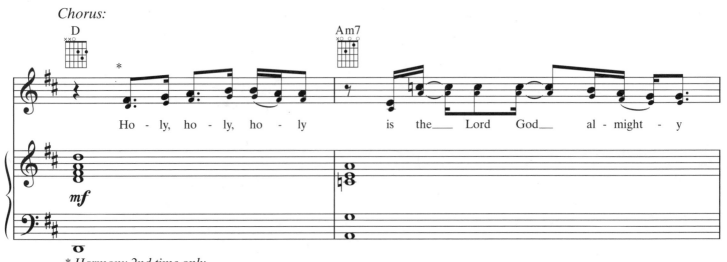

Ho - ly, ho - ly, ho - ly is the___ Lord God___ al - might - y

* *Harmony 2nd time only*

Repeat ad lib. and fade

SHOUT TO THE LORD

Words and Music by
DARLENE ZSCHECH

My Je - sus, my Sav - ior, Lord, there is none___ like You.___

___ All of my days___ I want to praise___ the won - ders of Your

might - y love. My Com - fort, my Shel - ter,

STRONGER

Words and Music by
BEN GLOVER, CHRIS STEVENS
and DAVID GARCIA

268

Bridge:

'Cause if He start-ed this work in your life, He'll be faith-ful to com-plete it if on-ly you be-lieve it. He knows how much it hurts, and I'm sure___ that He's gon-na help you get through___ this,___

Stronger - 9 - 6

STRONG ENOUGH

Words and Music by
MATTHEW WEST

Moderately slow rock ♩ = 80

(with pedal)

Verse 1 (sing 1st time only):

1. You__ must, you____ must think I'm strong__

Verse 2 (sing 2nd time only):

2. Well, may - be,____ may - be that's_ the point:____

Strong Enough - 6 - 1

274

275

Strong Enough - 6 - 4

UNTITLED HYMN
(Come to Jesus)

Words and Music by
CHRIS RICE

1. Weak and wound - ed sin - ner, lost and left to die, oh
2. Now your bur - den's lift - ed and car - ried far a - way. And

raise your head for love is pass - ing by. Come to Je -
pre - cious blood has washed a - way the stain. So sing to Je -

280

WE ARE

Words and Music by
ED CASH, CHUCK BUTLER,
JAMES TEALY and HILLARY McBRIDE

Moderate rock, half-time feel ♩ = 76

Verse 1:

1. Ev - 'ry se - cret, ev - 'ry shame,

ev - 'ry fear, ev - 'ry pain,

live__ in - side__ the__ dark,__ but that's not who__ we are.__

We Are - 7 - 1

284

We Are - 7 - 2

288

We Are - 7 - 6

VIA DOLOROSA

Words and Music by
BILLY SPRAGUE and NILES BOROP

Verse 1:

a Do - lo - ro - sa in Je - ru - sa - lem___ that day, the

sol - diers tried to clear___ the nar - row streets, but the

crowd pressed in___ to see the man___ con - demed___ to die___ on Cal - va -

ry. 2. He was bleed -

WHAT A SAVIOR

Words and Music by
JEREMIAH JONES

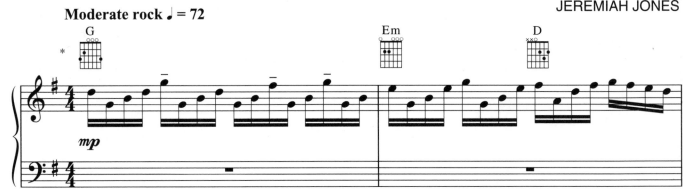

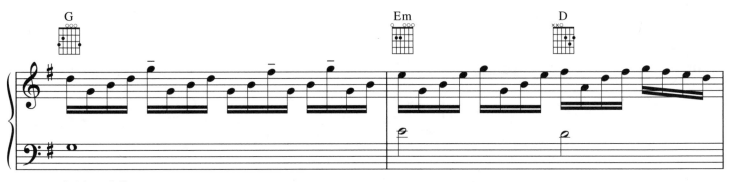

(with pedal)

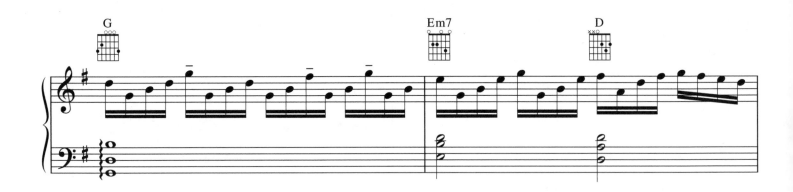

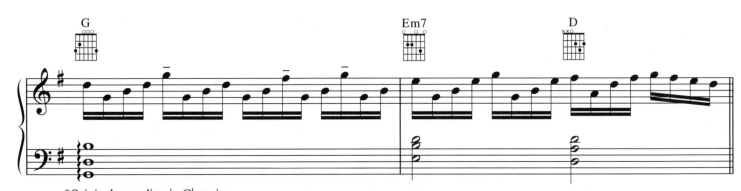

*Original recording in G♭ major.

What A Savior - 6 - 2

Hal - le - lu - jah! You are___ Sav - ior!___

Hal - le - lu - jah!___

You are___ Sav - ior!___

You are___ Sav - ior.___

WHEN I SAY I DO

Words and Music by
MATTHEW WEST

Moderately slow ♩ = 76

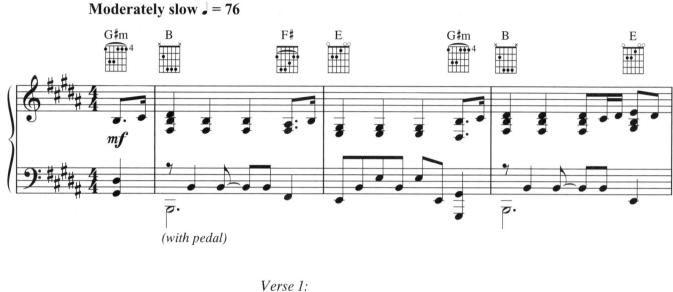

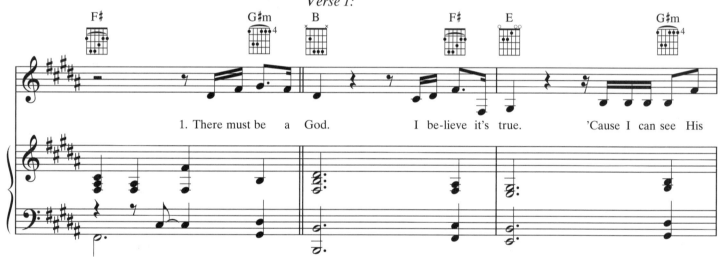

1. There must be a God. I be-lieve it's true. 'Cause I can see His

love when I look at you. And He must have a plan for this cra-zy

When I Say I Do - 6 - 1

YOUR GREAT NAME

Words and Music by
KRISSY NORDHOFF and MICHAEL NEALE

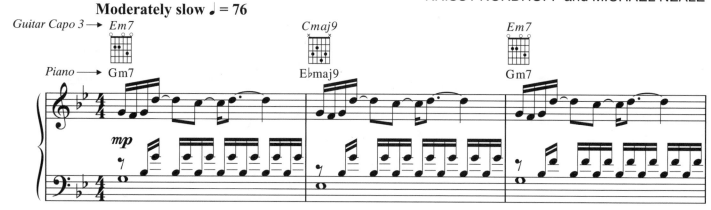

Verse 1:

1. Lost are____ saved,   find their____ way   at the sound____

____ of Your great name.   All con - demned____   feel no____

Your Great Name - 8 - 4

Your Great Name - 8 - 6

315

Repeat and fade

Your Great Name - 8 - 8

YOU RAISE ME UP

Words and Music by
ROLF LOVLAND and BRENDAN GRAHAM

You Raise Me Up - 5 - 1

317

You Raise Me Up - 5 - 2